Science and Religion

The myth of conflict

by
Professor Stephen M. Barr

*All booklets are published thanks
to the generous support of the members
of the Catholic Truth Society*

ignatius press · CATHOLIC TRUTH SOCIETY

LIGHTHOUSE CATHOLIC MEDIA
A NOT FOR PROFIT CORPORATION

CATHOLIC TRUTH SOCIETY
PUBLISHERS TO THE HOLY SEE

Contents

Three forms of conflict

It is often claimed that there is a conflict between religion and science. This claim takes three forms: historical, philosophical, and scientific.

The historical claim is that religious believers and institutions have been hostile to science and have tried to suppress it. This is powerfully symbolized, in the eyes of many people, by the Catholic Church's treatment of Galileo. And the impression is constantly reinforced in the public mind by the battles against Evolution waged by fundamentalist Protestant Christians.

The philosophical claim is that there is an *inherent* contradiction between the scientific and religious world-views. Science is based on reason and evidence, whereas religion is said to be irrational, because it is based on dogma, faith and mystery, which involve belief in things that cannot be seen and for which supposedly there is no evidence. Science is based on natural explanations and natural laws, whereas religion is based on miracles and the supernatural. Some people dismiss all religion as a matter of myth and magic, and therefore pure superstition, which is the very opposite of a rational scientific outlook.

The scientific claim is that the actual discoveries of modern science over the last four hundred years have debunked, or at least undermined, fundamental Christian beliefs about the universe and mankind's place in it. As the story is often told, science has dealt one blow after another to the religious conception of the world: Copernicus showed that man is not the center of the universe; Newton showed that the world is governed by blind and impersonal forces; modern astronomy has shown how small and insignificant we humans are compared to the cosmos as a whole; Darwin showed that humans differ only in degree from lower animals; and discoveries in fields such as neuroscience and Artificial Intelligence are beginning to show that the human "soul" is just the working of the brain, which is nothing but a complex biological computer.

It is the purpose of this booklet to show that almost all of these widespread notions are themselves myths with very little basis in fact. Indeed, in many cases, they are the very opposite of what history and science have to tell us.

The historical myth

The idea that the Christian religion, and the Catholic Church in particular, has opposed science and tried to hold it back is called by historians the "conflict thesis". Its roots lie in the contempt many thinkers of the Enlightenment had for revealed religion and for religious authority, and its growth was aided in the English-speaking world by anti-Catholic prejudice. Many historians of science trace the widespread acceptance of the "conflict thesis" to two enormously influential books published in late nineteenth-century America: *The History of the Conflict between Science and Religion*, by John William Draper, and *A History of the Warfare of Science with Theology in Christendom*, by Andrew Dickson White. These books have been thoroughly discredited by professional historians, who regard them as nearly worthless and filled with the grossest errors of fact and interpretation. And yet, the myth these books helped to create has become the "conventional wisdom" both for the general public and among scientists.

Here is what the myth says in broad outline: The tremendous progress made by the ancient Greeks in mathematics and science was halted by the rise of Christianity, which ushered in a dark age for learning that lasted a thousand years. Since Christians cared more about the next world than understanding this one, and more about the supernatural than the natural, they did not value science. Only when the West began to throw off the shackles of religion did science begin to revive, at which point it was set upon and persecuted by a hostile Church, as shown by the condemnations of Giordano Bruno in 1600 and Galileo in 1633. The overcoming of religious superstition and the development of a rational, scientific outlook accelerated during the Enlightenment. With Darwin came the decisive battle, which is still being bitterly fought.

This is the picture many people have, but as we shall see it is a fabric of falsehoods and misconceptions.

Church and science in ancient times

In the first place, Christianity had nothing to do with the decline of ancient Greek science and mathematics. They were in decline already by 200 BC. The last great Greek scientist of antiquity was the astronomer Ptolemy, who died around 165 AD, at which time Christians were still a small and persecuted sect with little influence on the wider culture. According to the distinguished historian of ancient science Prof. David C. Lindberg, the early Christians had no particular hostility to science, but had the same attitudes towards it as their pagan neighbors. (The oft-repeated story of Christians destroying the

Library of Alexandria with its wealth of pagan scientific treatises has no historical foundation. It is one of the many smaller myths from which the larger "conflict" myth has been constructed.)

Second, the idea that Jewish and Christian thought substituted supernatural explanations for natural ones is almost the reverse of the truth. It was the ancient pagan religions that saw the world as filled with occult and supernatural forces and deities of every kind - gods of ocean and earth, goddesses of sex and fertility, and so forth. Jews and Christians, by contrast, taught that there was only one God, who is not a part of nature or of its phenomena and forces, but *outside* of nature and indeed the very Author of Nature. This teaching to a great extent stripped the world of the supernatural, and allowed it to be seen more clearly as a *natural* world. To take one example, the Book of Genesis, which is so often misunderstood and mocked as mythological, was actually (in part) an attack on the supernaturalism and superstition of pagan mythology. When Genesis said that the Sun and Moon were mere "lamps" placed by God in the heavens, it was countering the religions that worshipped the Sun and Moon as divine. When it said that man (and only man) was made in the image of God and that he was to exercise "dominion" over the other animals, it was countering the religions in which men worshipped and bowed down to animals or to gods made in the image of animals.

For Jews and Christians, then, the world is not itself divine, but merely something created and governed by God. And since God is not capricious like the pagan deities, but creates and governs with wisdom, he has given the universe *laws*. Scripture and early Christian writings emphasize that God is the Lawgiver, not only to Israel and to mankind, but to the cosmos itself. In Jeremiah 33:25-26, for example, the Lord says, "When I have no covenant with day and night, and have given no laws to heaven and earth, then too will I reject the descendants of Jacob." Typical of early Christian writings is this passage from Minucius Felix written around 200 AD:

> "If upon entering some home, you saw that everything there was well-tended neat and decorative, you would believe that some master was in charge of it, and that he himself was much superior to those good things. So too in the home of this world, when you see providence, *order and law in the heavens and on earth*, believe that there is a Lord and Author of the universe, more beautiful than the stars themselves and the various parts of the whole world." [Emphasis added]

Even some non-religious scientists have suggested that belief in God, far from holding science back, may have helped create the expectation that nature, as the creation of a rational mind, is governed by intelligible principles and laws. For example, the eminent biologist E.O.

Wilson, himself a religious skeptic, explained in the following way why Chinese civilization, for all its scientific discoveries, did not produce a Newton or Descartes:

"[Chinese scholars] had abandoned the idea of a supreme being with personal and creative properties. No rational Author of Nature existed in their universe; consequently the objects they meticulously described did not follow universal principles. ... In the absence of a compelling need for the notion of general laws - thoughts in the mind of God, so to speak - little or no search was made for them."

The well-known cosmologist Andrei Linde, an avowed atheist, has suggested that the notion of a universe governed by "a single law in all its parts" is historically rooted in monotheism.

God, nature and the supernatural

The Christian faith does, of course, teach that there are "supernatural" realities, such as divine grace, that have an effect in the world. And yet, the word supernatural, which literally means "above the natural", would make no sense unless there is a "natural order" in the first place. In the same way, the concept of "miracles", which are extraordinary events that go beyond what is naturally possible, presupposes that there is a natural order that determines what is naturally possible and what is not. There is no logical contradiction between the idea of miracles and the idea of a lawful universe, for the same Lawgiver who established the laws of nature can also suspend them. Because he made the rules, he can make exceptions to them for the sake of some greater purpose. Nor has the belief in miracles held back the development of science in actual fact. As we shall see, the men who led the development of modern science in its first few centuries, the very men who were the pioneers in uncovering nature's laws, such as Isaac Newton, were for the most part devout Christians who believed in miracles.

There is much confusion today, unfortunately, among both religious people and atheists, about the relation of God to nature. Instead of seeing God as the "Author of

Nature", they see God and nature as somehow opposed or in competition. They seem to think that if something has a natural explanation, then God has nothing to do with it; and, conversely, if God is the cause of something it must be supernatural. Many religious people, therefore, look for evidence of God only in what is outside the course of nature or inexplicable by science, that is, in the gaps in our scientific understanding - hence the expression "the God of the gaps". And atheists think that by closing those gaps they will leave no place for God to hide.

The traditional Christian view is very different. It is that God, as the creator of the natural world, is the one who established its laws and gave to things their natural powers. Therefore evidence of God is primarily seen *in nature itself* and its ordinary processes, whose "power and working" reflect God's own power and wisdom. This is the message of the only biblical text that directly addresses science. The passage comes from the Book of Wisdom, composed about 100 years before Christ, and it speaks about the philosopher-scientists of ancient Greece, whom it reproaches for their spiritual blindness in failing to see evidence of God in the natural order that he has created:

"For all people who were ignorant of God were foolish by nature; and they were unable from the good things that are seen to know the one who exists, nor did they recognize the artisan while paying heed to his works;

but they supposed that either fire or wind or swift air, or the circle of the stars, or turbulent water, or the luminaries of heaven were the gods that rule the world. If through delight in the beauty of these things people assumed them to be gods, let them know how much better than these is their Lord, for the author of beauty created them. And if people were amazed at their power and working, let them perceive from them how much more powerful is the one who formed them. For from the greatness and beauty of created things comes a corresponding perception of their Creator. Yet these people are little to be blamed, for perhaps they go astray while seeking God and desiring to find him. For, while they live among his works, they keep searching, and they trust in what they see, because the things that are seen are beautiful. Yet again, not even they are to be excused; for if they had the power to know so much that they could investigate the world, how did they fail to find sooner the Lord of these things?" (*Ws* 13:1-9)

These words are prophetically relevant to those people today who "investigate the world" yet "fail to find" its author. Notice that the evidence of a Creator to which this passage points consists of phenomena that are perfectly natural: "fire," "wind," "swift air," "the circle of the stars," "turbulent water," and "luminaries of heaven [i.e. the stars, planets, Sun and Moon]."

The Letter of Clement, (circa a.d. 97), one of the oldest surviving Christian documents outside the New Testament (St Clement is listed as the third pope after St Peter), speaks of God's "ordering of his whole creation" and, again, points to natural phenomena:

> "The heavens, as they revolve beneath his government, do so in quiet submission to him. The day and the night run the course he has laid down for them, and neither of them interferes with the other. Sun, moon, and the starry choirs roll on in harmony at his command, none swerving from his appointed orbit. ... Laws of the same kind sustain the fathomless deeps of the abyss and the untold regions of the netherworld. Nor does the illimitable basin of the sea, gathered by the operations of his hand into its various different centers, overflow at any time the barriers encircling it, but does as He has bidden it. ... The impassable Ocean and all the worlds that lie beyond it are themselves ruled by the like ordinances of the Lord. ... Upon all of these the great Architect and Lord of the universe has enjoined peace and harmony."

Two ways in which God acts

Note the emphasis on the "laws" and "ordinances" by which God has guaranteed the order and harmony of the natural world.

In the Middle Ages, theologians distinguished two ways in which God acts in the world. He can act directly and in a supernatural manner (for example, turning water into wine), or he can accomplish his will through the operation of natural causes and processes. In the latter case, God is said to be the "primary cause", while the natural causes are said to be "secondary causes". As an analogy, consider the play *Hamlet*, in which the character Hamlet kills Polonius by stabbing him through a curtain. Why does Polonius die? Is it because Hamlet stabbed him or because Shakespeare wrote the play that way? Obviously, that's a silly question. *Both* are causes, but on different levels. Being stabbed through a curtain is the cause *within* the play, the "secondary cause", whereas Shakespeare is the "primary cause" in that he conceived of the whole play and everything in it, including Hamlet, Polonius, the knife, the stabbing, and Polonius dying. In an analogous way, everything that happens in the universe in accordance with the natural causes acting *within* it is fully the result of God's creative power as the "Author" of the universe. Although God does on extraordinary occasions "interfere" with nature - i.e. suspend its laws, or cause things to happen that would not occur naturally- he is equally the cause of what *does* occur naturally.

It has always been the Catholic view that while God can and sometimes does act outside the course of nature he *ordinarily* acts in and through nature. In the words of the great Scholastic theologian Francisco Suarez (1548-1617) "God does not interfere directly with the natural order where secondary causes suffice to produce the intended effect". This was also the teaching of St Thomas Aquinas (1224-1274) and other medieval theologians. This principle was important for science. It meant that when confronted by some puzzling event or new phenomenon, we should first look for natural explanations. Of course, it is not uncommon for superstitious people to see the supernatural in every unusual or strange event. But this tendency was strongly criticized by the great medieval scientist and theologian Nicole Oresme (1329-1392). In explaining marvels of nature, he said, "there is no reason to take recourse to the heavens … , or to demons, or to our glorious God, as if he would produce these effects directly, any more than [he directly produces] those effects whose [natural] causes we believe are well known to us." Another great scientist-theologian Jean Buridan (ca. 1300 - ca. 1358) said that when confronted by new phenomena we should seek "appropriate natural causes". This is why in our own day the Catholic Church does not declare a purported miracle to be worthy of belief until it has made great efforts to exclude the likelihood of natural explanations for it.

For Christians, then, God is indeed a cause, but not on the same level as natural causes. If we look for him on the same level, as though he were just another part of nature, we will fail to find him. It is this that leads atheists to think that

Christians believe "without evidence". For them evidence means either directly observing something with our five senses or deducing that something exists as a natural cause of what we observe (the way we observe smoke and deduce that there must be a fire). But God cannot be seen in these ways, for he is neither a part of the universe that could be directly sensed, nor a natural cause. Nevertheless, God is a cause: not a cause *within* nature, but the cause *of* nature. As with any cause, his existence can be inferred from the effects that he produces. The very fact that there is a universe at all - that there is *anything at all* rather than blank non-existence - calls for an explanation. And so do the magnificent harmony, order, and lawfulness that we see in the natural world, which testify to the mind of a rational Lawgiver.

God is not to be found in nature as a part of nature any more than Shakespeare is found in his plays as part of the scenery. But nature gives "evidence" of its Creator in the same way a play gives evidence of its author. As the Book of Wisdom put it, "from the greatness and beauty of created things comes a corresponding perception of their Creator." St Paul echoes this in his Epistle to the Romans, where he says about those who do not believe in God, "what can be known about God is plain to them, because God has shown it to them. Ever since the creation of the world his invisible nature, namely, his eternal power and deity, has been clearly perceived in the things that have been made." (*Rm* 1:19-20)

Church and science in the middle ages

When the barbarian invasions brought the Western
Roman Empire crashing down, a dark age began for
learning of all types, including science. People who know
history realize that the Church did not cause this dark age
but led the way out of it, not least by keeping literacy and
scholarship alive in the monasteries, and by copying and
recopying the precious and perishable manuscripts that
preserved the learning of the ancient world. But Western
Europeans in the Dark Ages (ca. 500 - ca. 1000)
possessed very few of the mathematical and scientific
books of antiquity. Around the eleventh century, however,
they began to acquire them through contact with the
Arabs and Byzantines, and became aware of the great
achievements of the ancient Greeks in these fields. A
hunger for this knowledge among both clergy and laity
led to an enormous effort to translate these works into
Latin. The medieval universities were founded as places
where this newly recovered knowledge could be studied.
These universities, the world's first, were Catholic
institutions. They were founded under Church auspices or
received Church patronage and protection, and were
staffed by clergymen. By the end of the middle ages,
there were about one hundred universities in Europe.

What we call "science" today was called "natural philosophy" at that time, and indeed well into the nineteenth century. One indication of how greatly the Catholic Church and her thinkers esteemed science is that in medieval universities the study of "natural philosophy" was a prerequisite for the study of theology. This esteem is all the more remarkable given the fact that the science they studied was of pagan Greek origin.

The medieval universities were the first institutions in human history where science was studied and taught on a continuous basis from generation to generation by a stable community of scholars. Before this, it had always depended on the whims of wealthy or powerful individuals. As the noted historian of science Prof. Edward Grant put it, the medieval universities "institutionalized" science. Moreover, they produced hundreds of thousands of graduates, who were introduced to scientific questions and from whose ranks scientific talent could emerge. The scientific community and scientific public created by the medieval universities were the soil in which the seeds of the Scientific Revolution germinated. Most of the great figures of the Scientific Revolution were educated in universities that had been founded in the Middle Ages.

What kind of science was done in medieval universities? It used to be thought that medieval science was stagnant and lacked creativity, with monkish scholars just repeating unquestioningly everything that Aristotle and other ancient authorities had said. That is why histories of science usually skipped from the ancient Greeks to Copernicus, as if nothing of consequence happened in between. However, thanks to the pioneering research of historians such as Pierre Duhem and A.C. Crombie, it is now accepted that medieval science had a great deal of vitality and originality.

Physics

Medieval scientists, such as Jean Buridan and Nicole Oresme, took important steps in physics, especially in the science of motion. They were the first to understand the important and subtle concept that an object could be speeding up at a constant rate (what physicists today call "uniform acceleration"). They proved the "Merton Theorem", which tells how far an object that is uniformly accelerating travels in a given time; and they speculated that falling objects obey this law. Three hundred years later, Galileo's brilliant experiments showed that this speculation was correct, and his Law of Falling Bodies was one of the first and most important steps in the creation of modern physics.

Optics

Breakthroughs were also made in optics (the science of light). Robert Grosseteste (1168-1253) applied geometry the study of light and formulated a law of "refraction" that was qualitatively correct. This allowed him to develop the correct theory of how lenses magnify images. Later in the thirteenth century, spectacles were invented, probably in Italy. This would lead to the invention (by spectacle makers) of the microscope and the telescope around the year 1600. It was also in the thirteenth century that the first mechanical clocks were invented, probably in England.

It is still not widely appreciated that the Middle Ages were a time of technological innovation. For example, the invention or improvement of the nailed horseshoe, the heavy plough, and other implements was of enormous economic importance. Water mills, although used in ancient times, were first used on a mass scale in the Middle Ages: the first energy revolution, which freed men from mere muscle power. The historian James Hannam writes, "These inventions catapulted medieval Europe into first place in the race to become the most technologically advanced civilization on earth. Although he did not know it, medieval man had already surpassed China, Islam, and the ancient world."

Human dissection

Another thirteenth-century breakthrough that was to have enormous implications for biology and medicine, was the introduction of human dissection in northern Italy. Hannam writes, "[This] is one of the most surprising events in the history of natural science. It was practically unheard of in any other culture [except ancient Egypt] due to strong taboos against cutting up bodies and not giving them the proper respect demanded by tradition." While the Catholic Church ought to get credit for its remarkably enlightened attitude in permitting this practice, quite the reverse is the case. As Hannam notes, "One of the most prevalent myths about the medieval Church is that it opposed human dissection."

A famous condemnation

Another myth concerns a famous Church "condemnation of science". In 1277, the bishop of Paris condemned 219 errors that he found in the writings of some Aristotelian philosophers. Several of these had to do with "natural philosophy" (i.e. Aristotelian science). At first glance, this looks like a direct attack by the Church on the freedom of scientific thought; but it was actually the opposite, as some historians have pointed out. Many things that had never been seen in nature were dismissed by Aristotelians as philosophically absurd and therefore absolutely impossible. For example, they thought they could prove by philosophical reasoning alone that a vacuum cannot exist. Not only weren't there any vacuums *in fact*, but even God himself, they said, could not have created a world in which there was a vacuum, nor could he by a miracle cause a vacuum to exist anywhere in this world.

It is *this* kind of thinking that the bishop of Paris rejected on the ground that it denied God's omnipotence. According to traditional Catholic teaching, unless something is a *logical* self-contradiction (such as a "four-sided triangle"), God has the power to create it. Other examples of things that the Aristotelians said were impossible even for God to create were other worlds besides this one or space that was not three-dimensional.

The condemnation of such ideas did not restrict freedom of thought, but expanded it and helped to enlarge the imaginations of medieval scientists. They began to ask themselves how a vacuum *would* behave if God were to create one, and to speculate about other worlds. Because "nothing is impossible for God" (as long as it does not involve a logical contradiction), the only way to settle the question of whether a certain kind of thing exists in the real world is by going out and *looking* to see what kinds of things God had actually chosen to create. The condemnations of 1277, if anything, favored an *empirical* approach to science, which is the modern approach, rather than an approach based on armchair reasoning. Modern physicists (just like the medieval natural philosophers) speculate about many wild possibilities that would have struck Aristotle and some of his followers as "absolutely impossible" - including, indeed, other universes and universes with more than three dimensions!

Some important medieval scientists

Most of the scientists of the Middle Ages were members of the Catholic clergy. Here are the most important ones:

Robert Grosseteste (1168-1253), mentioned earlier, was bishop of Lincoln. His combination of mathematical analysis and experiment in the study of light was an important step toward an empirical approach to science. (Cf. *Robert Grosseteste and the Origins of Experimental Science* by A.C. Crombie.) His student **Roger Bacon (ca 1214-1294)**, an English Franciscan monk, developed Grosseteste's ideas further. Although Roger Bacon probably never actually built a telescope or microscope, he predicted in his writings with amazing foresight that devices would be built that would make distant objects look near and small objects large.

St Albert the Great (1200-1280) was a German Dominican priest and later bishop. Most famous as the teacher of St Thomas Aquinas, St Albert helped introduce ancient Greek and Arabic science into the curriculum of medieval universities. He himself did observations and original work in botany and zoology, especially in the classification of plants, flowers, and fruits, in animal reproduction and embryology, and in the study of insects. The Dictionary of Scientific Biography calls his work *On*

Vegetables and Plants "a masterpiece for its independence of treatment, its accuracy and range of detailed description, its freedom from myth, and its innovation in systematic classification."

These three men, Robert Grosseteste, Roger Bacon, and St Albert, strongly emphasized in their writings the importance of an empirical approach to science.

Thomas Bradwardine (1290-1349), who became Archbishop of Canterbury, showed by a clever analysis that Aristotle's ideas on motion were mathematically inconsistent. He then did something never done before: develop a mathematical equation to describe how objects move in response to forces. Even though Bradwardine's law was not correct, it illustrates both the boldness and creativity of some medieval scientists and their willingness to criticize the mistakes of the science that they inherited from the ancient world.

Jean Buridan (ca. 1300 – ca. 1358), a priest and professor of the University of Paris, made important strides in the science of motion. Aristotle had taught that an object does not move unless an external force is acting on it. An arrow shot from a bow, for example, only keeps moving because the air keeps pushing on it. Buridan proposed the opposite (and correct) idea that when an object is set in motion it has something imparted to it, which he called "impetus", that keeps it in motion unless some external force acts to stop it. This was the forerunner of the modern physics concept of "momentum".

Nicole Oresme (1329-1392), a pupil of Buridan and later bishop of Lisieux, France, did work of genius in mathematics and physics. In mathematics, Oresme discovered the rules for combining "exponents" (even discussing fractional and irrational exponents!). He was the first to use graphs to plot physical quantities (three hundred years before Descartes!), and used them to prove the Merton Theorem about accelerated motion. Galileo later used diagrams very similar to Oresme's for the same purpose, which suggests that he was directly influenced by Oresme's ideas. (Books containing Oresme's diagrams were still in print in Galileo's time.) Oresme also argued that the apparent motion of the stars could be consistently explained by assuming the earth rotates on its axis, and he refuted common physical objections to this idea by analyses that were superior in some ways to those later given by Copernicus and Galileo.

Nicholas of Cusa (1401-1464) was a German Cardinal and an important figure in both the medieval Church and in medieval philosophy. For theological and philosophical reasons, he suggested that the universe is *infinitely* large, has *no center*, and that *all bodies* in it, including *both* the earth and the sun, are in motion. This was a far bolder and more modern conception of the universe than those proposed by Copernicus a century later and Galileo two centuries later.

The scientific revolution and priest-scientists

Although the Middle Ages paved the way for it, modern science did not really take off until the 1600s in what is called the Scientific Revolution. Because of the cases of Bruno and Galileo, many have the impression that modern science was founded in opposition to religion and that the founders of modern science saw themselves as rebels against the religious view of the world. Nothing could be further from the truth.

The great figures of the Scientific Revolution were mostly deeply religious men. Nicolaus Copernicus (1473-1543), whose theory that the earth went around the Sun sparked the revolution, was a church official (namely, a canon of Frauenberg Cathedral). Johannes Kepler (1571-1630), famous for his three great laws of planetary motion, announced the discovery of one of them with the words, "I thank thee, Lord God our Creator, that thou hast allowed me to see the beauty in thy work of creation." Galileo (1564-1642), despite his troubles with Church authorities, remained a devout Catholic throughout his life. René Descartes (1596-1650), whose work in mathematics was foundational for modern science, gave philosophical proofs of the existence of God. Blaise Pascal (1623-1662) was not only a mathematician and physicist of genius, but a religious mystic, who wrote his *Pensées* in defense of Christian belief against radical skepticism. Robert Boyle (1627-1691), considered the first modern chemist, left a large sum of money to endow a series of lectures whose purpose was to combat the ideas of "notorious infidels" (i.e. atheists). Isaac Newton (1643-1727), the greatest figure of the Scientific Revolution, spent as much time in theological and scriptural studies as he did on science. All of these men saw their work as showing the beauty of God's creation rather than as supporting atheism. (And this was true long beyond the 1600s. For example, the greatest physicists of the nineteenth century, Michael Faraday and James Clerk Maxwell, were deeply devout Christians.)

Where was the Catholic Church in all this? We all know about the condemnation of Galileo in 1633. What is much less known is the enormous positive role the Church played in scientific research and discovery from the 1600s to the present day. Prof. Lawrence M. Principe of Johns Hopkins University has written that "it is clear from the historical record that the Catholic Church has been probably the largest single and longest-term patron of science in history, ..."

One fact that dramatically illustrates this is the large number of Catholic priests who have made important discoveries in science and indeed founded whole branches of science. This story is a largely untold outside of scholarly books. Let us start with the century of the Scientific Revolution.

Priest-scientists of the 1600s

The Jesuit Order was founded in 1540, and within a few decades it was already in the forefront of scientific research, particularly astronomy. The "Gregorian Calendar", which the whole world uses today (promulgated by Pope Gregory XIII in 1582), was proposed by the Jesuit astronomer Christoph Clavius. Four other Jesuit astronomers of the 1600s deserve particular mention.

Christoph Scheiner (1573-1650) was one of several people who discovered sunspots with telescopes independently of each other. (The others were Galileo, Thomas Herriot, and Johannes and David Fabricius.) Galileo first figured out what sunspots were, but Scheiner made the most sustained and systematic observations of them. By tracking sunspots as they moved across the face of the sun, Scheiner discovered that the sun was rotating about a tilted axis. Scheiner's extensive sunspot data is still useful to scientists today.

Niccolo Zucchi (1586-1670) built the first reflecting telescope (which uses mirrors rather than lenses) in 1616, more than 50 years before Isaac Newton, who is usually given credit for this. In 1666, Cassini used data obtained by Zucchi with his reflecting telescope to show that Mars rotates about an axis.

Giambattista Riccioli (1598-1671) was the first astronomer to observe a "binary star". With Francesco Grimaldi, he made the first map of the moon's surface. (Thirty five of the moon's craters, including several of the largest, are named after Jesuit astronomers.)

Francesco Grimaldi (1618-1663) discovered, named, and made careful studies of the "diffraction" of light. 150 years later, this phenomenon was rediscovered and shown to prove that light is made up of waves. Diffraction is a fundamental effect important in every branch of physics. (Incidentally, the colored bands of light that one sees on CDs and DVDs are the result of diffraction.)

The Jesuits did not have all the glory. Four other priest-scientists of the 1600s helped to found entire branches of science:

Marin Mersenne (1588-1648) was a French priest of the Minimite Order. He is considered the founder of acoustics, because of his discovery of many of the basic facts about sound and vibrations. He discovered the law of the pendulum, one of Galileo's most famous discoveries, a year before Galileo did. He made fundamental contributions to the theory of reflecting telescopes. In addition, Mersenne played a key role in keeping scientists informed of each other's work. His convent became a meeting place of leading scientists, including Descartes, Fermat, and Pascal. In 1653, Mersenne organized the Academia Parisiensis (the Paris Academy), one of the first scientific organizations in Europe. The Dictionary of Scientific Biography calls Mersenne one of the "architects of the European scientific community".

Benedetto Castelli (1578-1643) was a Benedictine priest and student of Galileo. His book, *On the measurement of water currents*, began the modern study of hydraulics. His student Evangelista Torricelli was the first person to create a sustained vacuum, to discover the principle of the barometer, and to give the correct explanation of wind.

Buonaventura Cavalieri (1598-1647), a Jesuate (not Jesuit) priest was another student of Castelli's. Cavalieri's "method of indivisibles" was an important step toward the invention of Calculus later by Newton and Leibniz. Leibniz wrote, "In the most sublime geometry, the initiators and promoters ... were Cavalieri and Torricelli. Later others progressed even further, using their work."

Blessed Niels Stensen (Nicolaus Steno) (1638-1686) was a Danish Lutheran who converted to Catholicism and became a bishop. He did groundbreaking work in four branches of science: anatomy, paleontology, geology, and crystallography. His work as one of the leading anatomists in the world greatly increased knowledge of the glandular-lymphatic system. Stensen's duct, Stensen's gland, Stensen's vein, and Stensen's foramina are named after him. He also did important work on heart and muscle structure, brain anatomy, and embryology. But most important, he was the first person to give a detailed (and correct) theory of the origin of fossils, of sedimentary rock, and of geological strata, which began the scientific study of the history of the earth and revealed its enormous age. Therefore, among the founders of modern geology, he is usually listed first.

Important priest-scientists of later centuries

As science became more specialized, it became increasingly difficult to make fundamental contributions without years of technical training. As the priesthood also requires lengthy training, it is not surprising that the number of priest-scientists tended to decline over time. Nevertheless, in every century up to this day there have continued to be an astonishing number of important scientists who were Catholic priests.

Lazzaro Spallanzani (1729-1799) was one of the leading biologists of the eighteenth century. He investigated digestion, the dynamics of blood circulation, regeneration of limbs in lower animals, fertilization, respiration in plants and animals, and the senses of bats. He disproved the theory of "spontaneous generation" of life from non-living matter; and when Pasteur had to deal with the same question a hundred years later he based his famous experiments on those of Spallanzani.

René-Just Haüy (1743-1822) is regarded as the founder of the science of crystallography.

Giuseppe Piazzi (1746-1826) discovered the first asteroid, which he named Ceres, in 1801.

Bernhard Bolzano (1781-1858), a Czech priest, is an important figure in nineteenth century mathematics. He helped put Calculus on a more rigorous foundation. The "Bolzano-Weierstrass theorem" is one of the pillars of modern mathematics.

Pietro Angelo Secchi (1818-1878), a Jesuit, was one of the founders of modern astrophysics. He pioneered the use of spectroscopy to study the Sun and stars. His spectroscopic classification of stars is the basis of the one still used today. Perhaps nothing so dramatically symbolizes the positive relation of science and religion as the fact that Secchi did much of his groundbreaking research using an observatory built on the roof of Sant' Ignazio, one of the most beautiful churches in the city of Rome.

Gregor Mendel (1822-1884), an Augustinian monk, is famed for the experiments in plant breeding that led to his discovery of the basic mathematical laws of heredity. He is universally honored as the founder of the science of genetics.

Henri Breuil (1877-1961) was for decades one of the leading paleontologists in the world, and the foremost authority on cave paintings and prehistoric art.

Julius Nieuwland (1878-1936), a professor of chemistry at the University of Notre Dame, did work that led to the development of "neoprene", the first synthetic rubber.

Georges Lemaître (1894-1966), a Belgian priest-physicist, and the Russian mathematician Alexander Friedmann were the founders of the Big Bang Theory which is the foundation of modern cosmology.

We see that important priest-scientists existed in every century from the 1100s to the 1900s. They had many firsts to their credit and were the "founding fathers" of acoustics, hydraulics, geology, the study of fossils, crystallography, genetics, and Big Bang cosmology.

Has the church been a persecutor of scientists?

In the eight hundred years that the Catholic Church has been interacting with science, there is really only one case where she has condemned a scientist or scientific theory: Galileo and the heliocentric theory. Other supposed instances have been claimed by those who would like to show a pattern of persecution. Most well-known is the burning of Giordano Bruno at the stake in 1600, supposedly for suggesting that other inhabited worlds exist. In reality, Bruno was not a scientist so much as what we might nowadays call a "New Age mystic"; and it was his unorthodox theological ideas far more than his speculations about the universe that got him condemned.

Other claimed scientific martyrs at the hands of the Catholic Church are Roger Bacon in the 13th century, Bernhard Bolzano in the 19th, and Teilhard de Chardin in the 20th. None of these claims withstands scrutiny. Bacon spent time in prison, but there is no evidence that it had anything to do with his science. Bolzano ran into trouble with the political authorities in Vienna for his radical social and political views; but even though they pressured the Church to accuse him of heresy on those grounds, the bishops consistently refused and defended his orthodoxy.

And, finally, Teilhard de Chardin was indeed disciplined by the Vatican, but the Vatican explicitly stated at the time that it was *not* his scientific ideas that were at issue.

So the case against the Church comes down to Galileo, condemned to house arrest in 1633. Of course, the Church authorities did blunder badly in dealing with Galileo, but not out of hostility toward science or fear of it. They consulted leading astronomers and sincerely believed that they had science on their side. Nor were Galileo's scientific ideas *in themselves* all that important to the Church. The same ideas had caused no commotion when Copernicus first proposed them 90 years earlier. And a century before that, Nicolas of Cusa, a cardinal, had proposed much more radical ideas about the universe without causing alarm. But in Galileo's time the Church and society had been through the wrenching experience of the Protestant Reformation and its bloody aftermath, and the authorities were hypersensitive about new ways to interpret Bible passages.

The head of the Roman Inquisition in 1616 was Cardinal Bellarmine. In a famous open letter to one of Galileo's friends, the cardinal wrote: "If it were demonstrated that [the Sun were really motionless and the Earth in motion] we should have to proceed with caution in interpreting passages of Scripture that appear to teach the contrary, and rather admit that we do not understand them than declare something false which has been proven to be true." He went on to say, however, that he had "grave doubts" that such a proof existed and that "in case of doubt" one must stay with the traditional interpretations. And, in fact, a genuine "proof" that the earth moved was not available in Galileo's time. There were hints and plausible arguments, but really conclusive arguments were decades in the future. In 1758, at the urging of the famous Jesuit astronomer and physicist Rudjer Boskovic, Pope Benedict XIV removed the Church's censure from Copernican books (and, by implication, the Copernican theory itself for which Galileo had been condemned).

The church and evolution

Some people have the vague impression that the Catholic Church at some point condemned evolution. There is no truth to this. The Church made no official pronouncements about evolution for nearly a hundred years after Darwin published his theory in 1859. However, the general attitude of Catholic scholars and theologians toward evolution in the early days of the theory can seen from the *Catholic Encyclopedia*, which was written in the early 1900s. This was one of the outstanding products of Catholic scholarship at that time and received a "*nihil obstat*" and "*imprimatur*" certifying that it contained nothing contrary to Catholic doctrine. Its article entitled "Catholics and Evolution", after summarizing the theory, stated, "This is the gist of the theory of evolution as a scientific hypothesis. It is in perfect agreement with the Christian conception of the universe." A book called *The Question Box* published around the same time, gave responses to hundreds of common questions about the Catholic Faith. It sold millions of copies, and was used in Catholic schools. To the question, "May a Catholic believe in evolution?", it replied, "As the Church has made no pronouncement upon evolution, Catholics are perfectly free to accept evolution, either as a scientific hypothesis or as a philosophical speculation." The first Church pronouncement was by Pope Pius XII in his 1950 encyclical *Humani generis*. The pope stressed that the central point for Catholic faith is that the human spiritual *soul*, being non-material, is not the result of any physical or biological process, such as evolution (or for that matter sexual reproduction), but is conferred on each human being directly by God. As long as this is maintained, he said, Catholics were free to investigate the origin of the human body, including the theory that it evolved from the bodies of lower organisms, as long as they did so with prudence and care.

The greatest Catholic theologian of the 19th century is thought by many to be Blessed John Henry Newman. When Darwin published his theory, Newman immediately saw its scientific plausibility. Here is how

Newman's views were described by the eminent Catholic scientist Peter E. Hodgson,

"Newman [was] not concerned to consider the detailed scientific arguments for and against the theory of evolution. ... Instead, he simply remark[ed] that in its overall sweep it is far more plausible than the belief in special creation a few thousand years ago, a view that is still vigorously propagated [by fundamentalist Protestant 'creationists']. Such creationists, having rejected the authority of the Church as the Divine interpreter of Scripture, are trapped by the superficial meaning of the words, which inevitably leads them to a position that is antithetical both to theology and to science. Newman believed that the Creator lets His work develop through secondary causes, which have imparted 'certain laws to matter millions of ages ago, which have surely and precisely worked out, in the course of these long ages, those effects which He from the first proposed.' In a letter to Pusey, he addresses the same question: 'If second[ary] causes are conceivable at all, an Almighty Agent being supposed, I don't see why the series [of such causes] should not last for millions of years as for thousands.' Thus, "Mr. Darwin's theory *need* not be atheistical, be it true or not; it may simply be suggesting a large idea of Divine Prescience and Skill.""

For the Catholic Church, the physical processes by which plants and animals formed, like those by which stars and planets formed, are a matter of natural "secondary causes" and for the natural sciences, not theology, to concern themselves with.

Discoveries of science and Catholic belief

As noted in the Introduction, many believe that science has undermined fundamental Christian beliefs. At first sight, this seems strange, because science and Christian doctrine deal with different kinds of questions.

Science has to do with the natural causes of physical phenomena and with the structure and laws of the physical universe; whereas neither the Bible nor Catholic doctrine are directly concerned with such matters. In Scripture, natural phenomena such as rain and the growth of plants are ascribed to God's power, but not as a "theory" of those phenomena. Scripture does not offer detailed explanations of this or that physical effect, but rather teaches that all things reflect the wisdom of the Creator and exist by his power. Similarly, there have never been theories of natural phenomena proposed in Catholic catechisms, manuals of doctrine, or the decrees of councils and popes.

Sacred Scripture and the Catholic faith are not primarily concerned with the detailed workings of nature, but with higher things: God and man, love and truth, good and evil, sin and redemption - that is, with spiritual realities rather than physical phenomena. The distinction between the "spirit" and "matter" is basic. In Catholic theology, a spiritual being is one who has *intellect* and *will* and is therefore rational and free. In other words, a spiritual being is a *person*. God is a Spirit, Scripture tells us. And human beings, are made "in the image of God" because we have "spiritual souls." As St Irenaeus said in the second century, "Man is rational and therefore like God; he is created with free will and is master over his acts." It is the freedom of our intellect and will that makes us open to truth, goodness, and beauty, and that makes us capable of love.

So, it might seem that if science is concerned with matter and physical phenomena whereas religion is concerned with persons and spiritual reality, there would be little chance of a clash between them. But this is precisely where the sharpest conflict arises. The conflict, however, is not between the Catholic faith and science itself, but between the Catholic faith and a certain philosophy called "scientific materialism" that falsely claims to be the logical outcome of scientific discoveries.

Scientific materialism

Scientific materialism (also called "physicalism") says that nothing exists except matter governed by the laws of physics. This, of course, rules God out of existence, since the divine nature, according to Catholic teaching, is purely spiritual and has no materiality or physicality at all. It also rules out human "spiritual souls".

Why have the discoveries of science led so many people to embrace this philosophy? Surely the fact that natural science studies only physical phenomena doesn't mean that only physical phenomena exist. Part of the answer is that materialism is an "occupational hazard" of being immersed in the study of the material world. As the saying goes, "To the man with a hammer, everything looks like a nail." Psychologists tend to look for psychological explanations, political theorists for political ones, and economists for economic ones. Those in the physical sciences are prone to reduce everything to physical explanations. But there is more to it. Scientific materialists point to a number of aspects of the physical world that they think support their view.

Science has shown us a universe that is cold, uncaring, inhumanly vast, and governed by "blind, impersonal laws." This suggests to some people that religious believers are engaged in wishful thinking in imagining that a personal, loving being is behind it all. Christians, however, have never imagined that the physical universe cared about them or was personal in any way. The impersonality of the physical world may be an argument against pantheism or paganism, which see nature as a god or as filled with gods, but not against Judaism or Christianity, which sharply distinguish nature from God. And, as far as the laws of nature being "blind" and "impersonal", what else would they be? It is not the law that "sees" or is personal, but the Lawgiver.

The laws of nature

Here we get to a crux of the matter. Christians and scientific materialists have very different views of the laws of nature. As we saw, an ancient argument for the existence of God, found in the Bible and in Christian writings from the earliest times, is that the laws of nature give evidence of a divine Lawgiver. (This is one form of the ancient "argument from design".) For the scientific materialist, however, the laws of physics *in and of themselves* explain everything. So who is right? Do the laws of nature prove that God exists or that God is superfluous? We shall discuss this and explain why the materialist's view is unsatisfactory. We shall see that the discoveries of modern physics actually *strengthen* the ancient argument from design.

Explanations based on purpose

A second argument materialists make is that modern science has rejected explanations based on "purpose" and thereby undercut one of the main reasons for religious belief. It is easy to regard natural things as having purposes. For example, the Sun seems to exist to provide the energy that plants need to grow, and rain to provide the water. From this it is a short step to ascribing such purposes to a plan existing in the mind of God.

Aristotle's science was based on "teleology", the idea that natural processes and entities are directed toward "ends" or goals. According to Aristotle, heavy objects fall because their goal is to reach their natural or proper place at the center of the earth. The bodies of animals heal themselves of injury to reach the goal of bodily health and wholeness. But this teleological approach to science was set aside by the Scientific Revolution - especially in physics - and replaced by a "mechanistic" approach. Events were no longer seen as being drawn toward future goals, but as being driven along blindly by causes in the past and present. Modern physics explains how the Sun formed and how it generates energy without any reference to "ends". In the perspective of modern science, neither the Sun nor its energy are "for" anything, such as supporting life on earth; rather, life on earth takes advantage of the energy that just happens to be there. Darwinian evolution has pushed this mode of explanation further. To put it simply: trees do not exist so that monkeys can climb them; rather, some creatures adapted to the presence of trees by evolving the ability to climb.

We shall see however, that the idea of "purpose" in nature is by no means dead, and that it still makes sense to see the structure of the universe as being "for" the emergence of living beings, including ourselves. Interestingly, the evidence for this comes largely from physics and cosmology.

The human spiritual soul

A third argument of scientific materialists is that science has debunked the idea of the human spiritual soul. Computers have shown that machines can do many "mental" tasks, such as receiving information from sensory devices, analyzing or processing it, making decisions based on it, and storing it in memory. Neuroscience has shown how intimately our mental processes are connected with processes in the brain. Many have concluded that in the final analysis we are nothing but biochemical machines -"machines made of meat" or "wet computers" - and that our behavior is therefore entirely explicable by physics and chance. The supposed hallmarks of our spiritual natures, our moral and intellectual freedom, are increasingly said to be "illusions". We will see that some of the deepest discoveries of the twentieth century undermine this simplistic materialist view of the human mind.

God, the laws of physics and the design of the universe

Christians and other theists have always argued that the orderliness of the universe is the product of a mind. The atheist, on the other hand, argues that this orderliness is simply the result of the laws of physics. The Christian does not deny this, but says that those laws of physics were themselves the product of a mind.

Consider a simple analogy. Suppose one saw the chairs in a room arranged in neat rows and columns. The natural conclusion would be that someone had arranged them. That is analogous to the theist's position. The atheist's position is analogous to saying that chairs are arranged that way only because of a "law of chairs". Of course, there is a law of chairs, in the sense that the locations of the chairs fit a simple mathematical formula or rule. One could even use that rule to "predict" where the remaining chairs were if one only knew the locations of a few of them. But this "law of chairs" does not *explain* why the chairs in the hall have a pattern; it merely *states* the pattern with mathematical precision. The reason that the chairs obey this "law" or mathematical pattern is that someone imposed it.

48

The atheist, however, can point to natural objects that exhibit a similar kind of order with no one imposing it. The atoms of crystals, for example, are arranged in evenly spaced rows and columns much like the chairs in the room, and yet no "hand" arranged them; they spontaneously form themselves into those patterns by the operation of physical laws. Here blind laws do indeed seem to do the work of "designing". Or consider the "order in the heavens" to which early Christian writers such as Minucius Felix pointed as evidence of God. In particular, consider the fact that the planets all orbit the Sun in nearly the same plane, in the same direction, and approximately in circles. These features, we now understand, are the natural outcome when gravity makes a chaotically swirling cloud of gas and dust condense to form a star and planets. Newtonian physics has explained it. The even more remarkable patterns of planetary motion discovered by Kepler in the 1600s have also been adequately explained by Newtonian physics.

A deeper order

But *how* did Newtonian physics explain the beautiful orderliness of the solar system? It did so by appealing to a deeper order throughout the whole universe. It showed that Kepler's laws followed from more fundamental laws, namely Newton's laws of mechanics and gravity. But Newton's laws describe an order far grander and more impressive than the laws of Kepler! Order, in other words, was not explained away by Newton; quite the reverse. There was *more* order to explain after Newton made his discoveries than before. And so, we are led back to the same question: why is the grander order discovered by Newton there? Physics again has something to say: Newton's law of gravity comes from a yet more fundamental law, namely Einstein's laws of gravity (called "General Relativity"). But, lo and behold, the mathematical order in the universe described by Einstein's laws is even *more* splendid, beautiful and deep than that found by Newton! And the process continues: It is believed that Einstein's laws can in turn be derived from yet more beautiful and profound laws - very likely those of so-called "M theory" (or "superstring theory").

It is the same with the patterns seen in crystals. When a liquid crystallizes, the atoms go from milling around aimlessly to having an orderly pattern. But this order does not spring from mere disorder, as it may naively seem. When studied carefully, the orderly structure one finds in crystals is discovered to be the consequence of even *more* remarkable mathematical structure that exist at the levels of atomic and subatomic physics. Crystal structure can be described using relatively simple, geometry. The underlying structure found in the atomic and subatomic realm, however, require much more subtle and sophisticated mathematics. This deeper, hidden structure must be described using esoteric concepts such as spaces whose coordinates are "complex numbers" (i.e. they contain $\sqrt{-1}$), "Grassmann numbers" (which have the bizarre property that any such number times itself is zero), and all the strange and intricate mathematics of quantum mechanics.

As physicists have penetrated ever deeper into the inner workings of the physical world, they see an architecture based on ever richer and more refined mathematical ideas, ideas that it takes years of mathematical training to grasp.

All physicists can do is trace order to deeper order and laws to deeper laws. But that must end somewhere. Few theoretical physicists doubt that beneath it all there is a truly basic set of laws that govern all of physical reality. And history suggests that those most fundamental laws will turn out to be at least as mathematically rich and profound as anything discovered up to this time. If order calls for an explanation, then surely the magnificent order described by those fundamental laws calls for an explanation. But physics cannot provide it, for those ultimate laws cannot be traced to any deeper laws.

The mistake that the scientific materialist makes is to focus on the structures of *things* - such as crystals, solar systems, sunflowers, and seashells. *Those* structures can indeed be explained as arising by natural processes governed by laws. But the intricate structure of the *laws themselves* -

the *ultimate* laws of physics that govern all natural processes - obviously cannot be explained in that way.

In other words, science has not eliminated the question of why the universe is orderly and lawful. It has only showed us that the order and lawfulness of the universe runs far deeper and is far more impressive than anyone ever supposed. Such an order, based on ideas which takes the greatest efforts of the finest human mathematical minds to grasp, must surely originate in a mind far greater. That is why the famous astrophysicist and cosmologist Sir James Jeans remarked many years ago, "The universe begins to look more like a great Thought than a great machine."

Does nature have any purpose?

The scientific materialist has a point when it comes to "purpose" in Nature. Some of the arguments for it made in the past, especially in the eighteenth and nineteenth centuries, have come to seem naïve in the light of the insights of Darwinian biology. Purpose is often revealed by the way the parts of a thing or a system work together harmoniously for some end. The parts of organisms work together in this way, as do the parts of individual organs, such as the human eye, or of entire ecosystems. But much, if not all, of this biological purposefulness can be explained by adaptation and by the trial-and-error process called natural selection. As was said above, from the viewpoint of science it was not that trees were put there for monkeys to climb, but that some creatures adapted to the presence of trees by evolving the ability to climb.

While all this is true, there are limits to the kinds of environments living things can adapt to. Life can adapt to arid climates, but if water did not exist *at all* none of the life we know of could exist. Life can adapt to places with little or no sunlight, but if the Sun and stars did not exist *at all* none of the life we know of could exist. (All known life is ultimately dependent on energy that is traceable back to the Sun or other stars. Even the geothermal energy that supports some life in the ocean depths derives from radioactivity in the earth, which was originally stored up in those radioactive elements by nuclear processes that went on in stars and supernovas before our Sun was born.)

In other words, there are some minimal conditions that a universe must satisfy for life to be possible within it. For example, it has to contain suitable building blocks (such as water) that could be combined into stable and complex structures; it has to have sources of energy (such as the Sun); and it has to last long enough so that there is enough time for life to evolve and for the complex processes of life to occur. And the fact that our universe satisfies these conditions is due to the laws of physics having very special features.

Anthropic coincidences

Over the last few decades, it has been discovered that there are many respects in which the laws of physics of our universe are "just right" to make life possible. These are called "anthropic coincidences" ("anthropos" means "human being" in Greek).

Here are a few examples:

(1) If the world did not obey the principles of quantum mechanics, atoms and molecules would not be stable building blocks with well defined properties out of which living things could be built.

(2) If the electromagnetic forces between particles were significantly stronger than they are, the electric repulsion within atomic nuclei would blow them apart, except for the nuclei of the very lightest elements.

(3) If the so-called "strong force", which holds nuclei together, were even a small fraction weaker than it is, a crucial nucleus called deuterium could not exist, and the nuclear reactions that power the Sun and similar stars would not take place - depriving earth of the energy needed for life. Moreover, these same nuclear reactions involving deuterium are needed to initiate the chain of reactions that form all the elements of the Periodic Table (except hydrogen). Without them, the only element in nature would have been hydrogen, rather than the rich palette of elements needed for life. (Twenty-five elements are found in the human body.)

(4) Neutrons are very slightly heavier than protons. Had it been the other way around, isolated protons would be unstable and hydrogen would not exist (though other elements could). Almost all organic molecules contain hydrogen, so life would probably not exist.

(5) If the number of extended dimensions of space were greater than three, gravity would act differently and would not allow planets to orbit stars - they would either plunge into the stars or fly off into space.

(6) If a parameter called the cosmological constant were not fantastically small (about 10^{-120}), the universe would not have lasted the billions of years needed for life to evolve, but would have collapsed or blown apart in only a tiny fraction of a second.

There are many such "coincidences". Some involve certain "constants of nature" (numbers appearing in the laws of physics) having to be "fine-tuned" very precisely to special values for life to exist. This gives every appearance that the rules by which the universe was put together were chosen to make life possible. This would be a clear indication of purpose.

There is an alternative way to explain these coincidences. It is conceivable that the fundamental laws of physics have a flexibility that allows some of these "constants of nature" and other features of the world that have been thought to be fixed and unchanging (such as the types of forces and their strengths, the types of particles and their properties, the number of space dimensions, and so forth) to vary from region to region of the universe. This is the so-called "multiverse" idea. The idea is that so many different possibilities have been "tried out" in different regions of the multiverse, as it were, that it was inevitable that in *some* place these variable features were "just right" for life to exist. This is an interesting idea, and may very well be right. There are theoretical reasons for taking it seriously. However, even if it is right, it does *not* dispose of the evidence for purpose. The point is that only if the fundamental laws of physics were very special indeed would they lead to a multiverse. So, one way or another, the laws of nature had to be very special for us to be here.

This is a good place to make a comment about the "inhuman" vastness of the universe. If the universe were not so vast, it would not contain life. The laws of gravity relate the size of the universe to how long it lasts. A universe has to last a long time to allow life to evolve - on earth it took billions of years. But, according to Einstein's theory, unless the universe gets to a size of *at least* billions of light-years, it will not last billions of years. In fact, if the universe never got bigger than a billion miles across, it would only last a couple of hours. In other words, even the vast size of the universe, which many take to be a sign of our "insignificance", is actually a condition for our being here, and so can be seen as further evidence that we were part of the plan and purpose of the world's existence.

Science and the human spiritual soul

For about 250 years physicists believed that the universe runs like clockwork. The laws of physics rule with an iron grip. Everything that happens in the physical universe is uniquely and inevitably determined by what happened in the past. The technical way to say this is that the laws of physics are "deterministic". That seemed a death blow to the idea of human free will. For if "physical determinism" were true our bodies and brains would be as rigidly controlled by the laws of physics as everything else in the physical world. And if human beings are not morally and intellectually free, then we are not "spiritual" beings, in the Catholic meaning of the term, but merely robots.

In the 1920s, however, there was a radical rethinking of the foundations of physics. The old "classical" framework was replaced by the framework of quantum mechanics. Quantum mechanics is *not* deterministic. In most physical situations, the laws of physics allow more than one outcome (in fact, typically a virtually infinite number of them). For example, a radioactive nucleus or an unstable particle can decay at *any* time; the laws of physics only prescribe the *probability* that it will decay within a given time period (e.g. it has a 50% chance of decaying within its "half life"). This does not prove that there is free will, or say how free will "works". But it does mean that there is no rigorous argument against free will based on the iron rigidity of the fundamental laws of physics, as many people once thought. Nevertheless, the belief that free will is incompatible with the laws of physics is still very strong among philosophers.

Quantum mechanics has other profound implications. It seems to say that mind and consciousness are as fundamental a part of reality as physical systems and matter are. As traditionally understood, quantum mechanics distinguishes between physical "systems" and conscious "observers" of those systems (including human beings). The reason for this, roughly speaking, is the following. As mentioned, quantum mechanics deals in *probabilities*. Probabilities have to do with what someone *knows* or doesn't know. (The more you know the less you have to rely on probabilities.) The one who knows or doesn't know has traditionally been called "the observer" in quantum mechanics. And to know requires a *mind* and *consciousness*.

Heisenberg himself said, for example, that the mathematics of quantum mechanics "represents no longer the behavior" of physical systems but "rather our knowledge of their behavior". And Sir Rudolf Peierls, a leading twentieth century physicist, said, "the quantum mechanical description is in terms of knowledge, and knowledge requires *somebody* who knows." The Nobel Prize winning physicist Eugene Wigner, commented that "the very study of the physical world led to the conclusion that the content of the consciousness is an ultimate reality."

Moreover, a line of argument that goes back to the great mathematician John von Neumann says that the mind of the observer is not completely describable by physics within the framework of quantum mechanics. Here is Peierls again: "the premise that you can describe in terms of physics the whole function of a human being ... including its knowledge and consciousness is untenable." This is why Wigner stated that "materialism" is not "logically consistent with present quantum mechanics."

It seems that there is only one way to escape such conclusions, and that is through something called the "Many Worlds Interpretation" of quantum mechanics. In the traditional interpretation of quantum mechanics, there are many possible outcomes in a typical physical situation, but only one actually happens. (So probabilities come into the discussion, and with them knowledge and minds.) But in the Many Worlds Interpretation, *all* the possible outcomes happen, but in different "worlds" or branches of reality. Reality is therefore constantly splitting into branches - an infinite number of them. That means that everybody, including *you*, exist in an infinite number of copies. And these copies are living all the possible lives allowed by the laws of physics! This is too much for most physicists to swallow. It seems, however, that if one takes the materialist (or physicalist) view that the laws of physics describe everything, one is forced to accept the Many Worlds picture.

Another discovery that undercuts the materialist view of the human mind is a revolutionary theorem in mathematics proved in 1931 by the great Austrian logician Kurt Gödel. What Gödel's Theorem showed is that there is more to doing mathematics and discovering mathematical truth than mechanically following rules - the way a computer does, for instance. From this some have argued that the human mind, at least when thinking mathematically, is not just operating like a machine. The philosopher John R. Lucas of Oxford University wrote in 1961, "Gödel's Theorem seems to me to prove that Mechanism is false, that is that minds cannot be explained as machines. So also has it seemed to many other people: almost every mathematical logician I have put the matter to has confessed to similar thoughts ... ." Lucas developed a careful argument for this conclusion. Since the 1980s, this Gödelian argument has been further refined and vigorously defended by the eminent mathematician and mathematical physicist Sir Roger Penrose, also of Oxford University. The same view was held by Gödel himself, who in fact called materialism "a prejudice of our time". A point that Gödel, Lucas, and Penrose all emphasize is that the human mind is capable of doing something that mere computing machine cannot, namely *understanding concepts* and grasping *meaning*.

Most scientists would be skeptical of the anti-materialist arguments based on quantum mechanics or Gödel's Theorem. Nevertheless, these arguments have been advanced and defended by some of the most brilliant scientific and mathematical minds of the twentieth century. One thing therefore is clear: materialism is definitely *not* a conclusion to which modern science necessarily leads.

The Big Bang, the beginning and creation

As atheists often tell the story, Copernicus and Galileo overthrew, or at least unsettled, the Christian view of the universe, which was that man dwells at the very center, as befits the only creature made in the image of God. The truth, however, is quite different. The medieval picture of the cosmos, in which there were transparent celestial spheres rotating around a centrally located and spherical earth, did not come from any Jewish or Christian source, but from ancient Greek science, specifically Aristotle and Ptolemy. (The Old Testament Jews, like their Near Eastern neighbors, had the older, more primitive conception of a flat earth supported by pillars and covered by a dome-like sky or "firmament".) Moreover, neither the ancient Greeks nor the medieval Christians who borrowed their astronomical ideas saw the center of the universe as being the most glorious place. The center of the universe was for both the *lowest* place; the farther a thing was from it the more exalted it was in every way. Man dwelt in an intermediate position, neither in the dismal underworld nor in the splendid heavens.

Jews and Christians have always based their cosmology (or picture of the universe) on the science or commonly held ideas of the time. There was, however, one point of the cosmology of Jews and Christians that set them apart from the pagan peoples among whom they lived. It was not about space and whether it had a center, but about time and whether it had a beginning.

A beginning

The philosophers of ancient Greece, including Plato and Aristotle, believed that the world had always existed. It was the Bible - indeed, its very first words - that introduced the idea of a "Beginning" into Western thought. The pagans often ridiculed the Jews and Christians for this idea, asking them what their God was doing for all that infinite time before he finally got around to making the world. St Augustine (354-430) had a profound answer. He said that it made no sense to ask what God was doing "before" he made the universe, because there was no such thing as a time "before the universe". He pointed out that time, as a feature of the created world, is *itself* something created. Therefore, time can only exist *after* creation has taken place, not before. Indeed, the very idea of "before" creation is meaningless. As St Augustine put it, "Why do they ask what God was doing 'then'? There was no 'then' where there was no time." In other words, *the beginning of the universe was also the beginning of time itself*. Both the Fourth Lateran Council (1215) and the First Vatican

Council (1870) spoke of God creating the world "from the beginning of time".

For centuries, modern science found no evidence of a "Beginning". In Newtonian physics, it was natural to think of time, like space, having no limits. In the nineteenth century, physicists discovered the law of "conservation of energy", which says that "energy can neither be created nor destroyed". Chemists found that the amount of matter does not change in chemical processes; so matter too could neither be created nor destroyed. Almost every indication from science was that matter, energy, time, and space had always existed and always would. Consequently, many scientists came to believe that the ancient pagan philosophers were right and that the world had always existed. This was the view of most American physicists and astronomers even as late as 1959, according to one survey. The idea of a Beginning was seen by many of them as an outdated religious myth.

The Big Bang theory

However, things began to change when Einstein proposed his theory of gravity ("General Relativity") in 1916. In the 1920s, a Russian mathematician named Alexander Friedmann and a Belgian physicist named Georges Lemaître (who was also a Catholic priest) found solutions to the equations of Einstein's theory that described a universe in which space itself is expanding. In 1927, Fr

Lemaître proposed that the universe had started off as an extremely small dense ball, which he called the "primeval atom", which exploded and expanded to form the vast universe we see today. This came to be called the Big Bang Theory. Scientists were very slow to accept this theory, in part because they found the idea of a beginning hard to swallow. But in 1964 it was discovered that the universe is filled with faint radiation (called the "cosmic background radiation"), which turned out to be the afterglow of the Big Bang explosion. Since then, the evidence in favor of the Big Bang Theory has grown so strong that now few scientists seriously doubt it.

Was the Big Bang the beginning of the universe? Possibly not. Some interesting theories have been proposed in which the Big Bang was only the beginning of one phase of the history of the universe. But there are very strong theoretical physics arguments (based on the Second Law of Thermodynamics and on some theorems proved by the physicists Borde, Guth and Vilenkin a few years ago) that suggest that the universe must have had a beginning at *some* point, whether it was the Big Bang or some earlier point.

Moreover, physics says that the beginning of the universe was also the beginning of time itself. Physics came to this conclusion by an argument very similar to the one St Augustine used 1,600 years earlier. St Augustine started with the idea that time is something *created*. Modern physics starts with the idea that time is something *physical*: "space-time" according to Einstein's theory is a physical fabric that can stretch, bend, and vibrate. So time, being a feature of the physical universe, can only exist after the universe begins. St Augustine's famous reply to the pagan scoffers has been vindicated. So profound were St Augustine's insights that it is common for technical research papers on "quantum cosmology" to quote his writings on the nature of time.

Creation

In recent decades, some physicists have suggested that science will someday be able to explain the Beginning, possibly through the idea of "quantum creation of universes". In a certain sense, that may be true. That is, the Big Bang (or the Beginning, whenever it was) may have been "natural" in the sense that it obeyed the laws of nature. It is quite possible that the fundamental equations of physics correctly describe everything that happened at the beginning of the universe. Would that be the same as "explaining creation"? Would that mean that no Creator was necessary? No. That is confusing two ideas. Let us go back to the analogy of a play. The "beginning" of the play *Hamlet* consists of its first words in Act I, Scene I. One may explain this beginning - i.e. why the play begins in a particular way, with particular words - by the laws of English grammar, by the principles that govern the proper writing of plays, by the way the opening scenes fit into the play's overall plot, and by various other factors. But while all these things may explain why the play begins as it does, they do not explain *why there is a play at all*. The reason there is a play at all is that William Shakespeare decided to write one and conceived it in his mind.

Science may discover the ultimate laws of physics (it may already have, if M theory turns out to be correct). And it is quite possible that the mathematics of those laws might require that any universe described by them have a beginning and that its beginning happen in a certain way. But that would still not tell us why there actually exists a universe described by those laws - rather than no universe at all or a universe described by other laws. A story may tell of real events or of fictitious events; and the mere fact that a story tells of something beginning does not mean anything really does begin except in the story. Similarly, a set of mathematical equations may describe a really existing universe or a fictitious one; and the mere fact that they might describe a universe that has a beginning does not make them a description of anything real. What gives *reality* to the universe is not the equations that describe its structure, but God, who is the ultimate reality and source of being.

Extraterrestrial life

Many people ask whether the existence of intelligent extraterrestrial life would be a problem for Catholic theology. Would such beings have spiritual souls? Would they be made in the image of God? Would they need to be redeemed, and if so how could the Incarnation happen for them? If God became man, how can he also become another type of creature, or even many other types? How can Christ be several kinds of being and yet be the same person? There is really no problem. If extraterrestrial creatures of some species have reason and free will, then they also have spiritual souls and are made in the image of God. If that species "fell" it would need redemption. And nothing prevents multiple Incarnations of the Son of God. In his earthly Incarnation, God the Son "assumed" a human nature. He remained one divine Person, but operated in two modes, as it were. No less a theologian than St Thomas Aquinas argued that it was possible for the Son to "assume" several human natures, i.e. have several human Incarnations. (See *Summa Theologiae*, Part III, Question 3. Article 7). If the Son could assume multiple natures, there is no reason why they could not be any rational and free natures and not just human natures.

Recommended reading

Books by Scientists:

Stephen M. Barr, *Modern Physics and Ancient Faith* (2003). [An in-depth discussion of the theories of modern physics showing their consonance with traditional religious conceptions, accessible to the scientific layman.]

Peter E. Hodgson, *Science and Belief in the Nuclear Age* (2005), *Theology and Modern Physics* (2006). [Lucid essays by an eminent Catholic nuclear physicist who was a professor at Oxford.]

Francis S. Collins, *The Language of God: A Scientist Presents Evidence for Belief* (2007). [A powerful defense of religious belief and account of his own conversion to Christianity by an eminent geneticist. N.B. The appendix defends views on medical ethics incompatible with Catholic teaching.]

Owen Gingerich, *God's Universe* (2006). [Gingerich is professor emeritus at the Harvard-Smithsonian Center for Astrophysics.]

John C. Polkinghorne, *The Faith of a Physicist* (1996). [Polkinghorne is a former professor of theoretical particle physics at Cambridge University who became an Anglican clergyman.]

Books on the Catholic Church and Science:

James Hannam, *The Genesis of Science: How the Christian Middle Ages launched the Scientific Revolution* (2011). [A very lively account of the Catholic Church's involvement in science in the Middle Ages.]

Edward Grant, *The Foundations of Modern Science in the Middle Ages: Their Religious, Institutional and Intellectual Contexts* (1996). [An important and readable book by a leading historian of science.]

Alan Cutler: *The Seashell on the Mountaintop: A Story of Science, Sainthood, and the Humble Genius who Discovered a New History of the Earth* (2003). [A biography of Blessed Niels Stensen that has a balanced perspective on historical relation of science and religion.]

Ronald L. Numbers, *Galileo Goes to Jail and Other Myths about Science and Religion* (2009). [The relevant chapters are 1, 2 ,5, 6, 7, 10, 11.]

Christopher T. Baglow, *Faith, Science, and Reason: Theology on the Cutting Edge* (2009). [An excellent textbook for high-school or college students.]

Creation & Science
Has science eliminated God?

Who created the Universe? Is a creator even necessary? Can science explain how the Universe came into being without reference to a creator God? This booklet explores these ideas and the arguments that have been brought into sharp focus by Stephen Hawking's claim that his cosmological model 'left nothing for a creator to do'. Dr Carroll examines the Church's teaching on creation from Augustine and Aquinas to the present and explains why without a creator God, science itself would not exist.

Dr William Carroll is Aquinas Fellow in Theology and Science at Blackfriars, University of Oxford.

ISBN: 978 1 86082 714 3
CTS:EX36-P
www.ignatius-cts.com

COSMIC ORIGINS

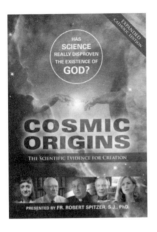

This fascinating film features **Fr. Spitzer** and a group of physicists and academic heavyweights exploring modern scientific theories about how the universe came to exist. Joining Fr. Spitzer are Nobel Laureate **Arno Penzias** (who discovered the background radiation from the Big Bang), Templeton Prize winners **John Polkinghorne** (Cambridge) and **Michael Heller** (Vatican Observatory), **Owen Gingerich** (Harvard), **Lisa Randall** (Harvard), **Jennifer Wiseman** (NASA) and **Stephen Barr** (University of Delaware), who narrates the film. Throughout the journey, viewers learn that modern scientific paths point toward a very Christian understanding of how we came to be.

DVD CO-M . . . 49 min., $19.95

ignatius press
www.ignatius.com • 1-800-651-1531

Handbook of Catholic Apologetics
Reasoned Answers to Questions of Faith

Peter Kreeft and Ronald Tacelli

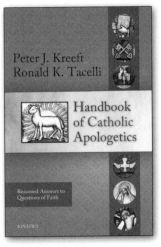

This is the only book that categorizes and summarizes all the major arguments in support of the main Christian beliefs. Also included is a treatment of Catholic-Protestant issues, showing how Catholicism is the fullness of the Christian faith. This is an informative and valuable guidebook for anyone looking for answers to questions of faith and reason.

HCATA-P . . . 600 pp, Sewn Softcover, $21.95

ignatius press
www. ignatius.com · 1 (800) 651-1531